DENG AKOL JUACH
PhD Language and Linguistics

A Note from the Publisher

The publisher wishes to acknowledge and thank Dr Douglas H. Johnson for his invaluable help and support for Africa World Books and its mission of preserving and promoting African cultural and literary traditions and history. Dr Johnson and fellow historians have been instrumental in ensuring that African people remain connected to their past and their identity. Africa World Books is proud to carry on this mission.

© Deng Akol Juach, 2020

ISBN: 978-0-6487937-1-7

All rights reserved. No part of this publication may be reproduced, stored in a retrieval system, or transmitted, in any form, or by any means, electronic, mechanical, photocopying, recording or otherwise, without the prior permission of the publishers.
This book is sold subject to the conditions that it shall not, by way of trade or otherwise, be lent, re-sold, hired out or otherwise circulated without the publisher's prior consent in any form of binding or cover other than in which it is published and without a similar condition including the condition being imposed on the subsequent purchaser.
Africa World Books Pty. Ltd.

Design and typesetting: Africa World Books

Dedication

This book is dedicated to the memory of my maternal uncle, Jok Dut Jok, who took me to school at an early age in a village called Pariak.

Acknowledgements

I want to thank my colleagues, relatives, and friends for their contributions, technical advice, and encouragement in the writing of this book.

Table of Contents

Dedication 3
Acknowledgements 3
Abstract 11
Preface 13
Chapter One 15
Introduction 15
1.1 Language, Performance, and Placement 17
1.1.1 Language 17
1.1.2 Performance 17
1.1.3 Testing 17
1.1.4 Placement Testing 18
1.1.5 Language Testing 18
1.2 Language Testing in China 24
1.3. Proficiency 28
1.3.1 Language Proficiency 28
1.3.2 English Language Proficiency and Academic English Language Proficiency 29
1.3.3 English Language Proficiency and its Relation to Academic English 30
1.3.4 Foreign Language Proficiency 30
1.3.5 Foreign Language Proficiency Guidelines . 31
1.3.6 Communicative Language Proficiency 31

1.4 English Language Proficiency Tests 32
1.4.1 Idea Proficiency Test Results 33
1.4.2 Maculattis Assessment of Competencies Test of English Proficiency 33
1.4.3 Stanford English Language Proficiency 34

Chapter Two 35
Variable Placement Tests 35
2.1 Placement Testing 35
2.2 Global Placement Test 36
2.3 Placement Tests as an Adaptive Tests .. 37
2.4 Placement Testing as an Essential Ingredient 38
2.5 Who Should Be Tested? 39
2.6 Placement Test Selection 39
2.7 Test and Testing 40
2.7.1 Tests 40
2.7.2 Tests and Examinations 42
2.7.3 Direct and Indirect Tests 43
2.7.4 Subjective and Objective Tests 44
2.7.5 Tests and Quizzes 45
2.7.6 Oral and Written Tests 46
2.7. Objective Tests 48
2.7.8 True or False Tests 48

2.7.9 Multiple-Choice Tests 48
2.7.10 Matching Tests 49
2.7.11 Norm-Referenced Test versus Criterion referenced Test 49
2.7.12 Indirect Tests versus Direct Tests 50
2.7.13 Discrete Point Tests versus Integrative Tests 51

2.8 Testing 52
2.8.1 Testing Language for Specific Purposes 52
2.8.2 Testing Methods 53
2.8.3 Testing Grammar 54
2.8.4 Testing Vocabulary 55
2.8.5 Testing Reading Comprehension 56
2.8.6 Testing Oral Ability 57
2.8.7 Testing Writing 60

Chapter Three 61
Test Qualities 61
3.2 Measurement and Evaluation 64
3.2.1 Measurement 64
3.2.2 Evaluation 64
3.3 Testing and Evaluation 65
3.4 Assessment and Evaluation 66

3.4.1 Assessment 66
3.4.2 Evaluation 67
3.5 The Test Development Process 68
3.5.1 Design 68
3.5.2 Operationalisation 68
3.5.3 Administration 69
3.6 Modern Trends in Language Testing 69
3.7 Uses of Language Tests in Educational Programs 70
3.8 Classification of Tests 71
3.9 Characteristics of a Good Test 72
3.9.1 Validity 72
3.9.2 Reliability 74
3.9.3 Discrimination 75
3.9.4 Backwash 75
3.9.5 Objectivity 76
3.9.6 Scorability 76
3.9.7 Practicability 76

Chapter Four 80
Other Variable Types of Tests Used in Language Testing 80
4.1 Achievement Tests 80
4.2 Language Aptitude Tests 81

4.3 Diagnostic Tests 82
4.4 Progress Tests 82
4.5 Formative Tests 82
4.6 Summative Tests 83
4.7 Essay Tests 83
4.8 Hypothesis Tests 83
4.9 Subtests 84
4.10 Test-Retest Reliability 84
4.11 TOEFL Tests 85
4.12 Problems in Language Testing 85
  4.12.1 Problem 1 85
  4.12.2 Problem 2 85
  4.12.3 Problem 3 86

Chapter Five 87
Samples of Tests 87
5.1 English Placement Test 87
5.2 English Proficiency Test 111
  5.2.1 English Grammar: Part I 111
  5.2.2 English Grammar 115
  5.2.3 English Vocabulary 120
  5.2.4 English Reading Comprehension 123

Summary and Conclusion 129

References 131
Appendices 135
　Appendix A: Types of English Proficiencies Used in This Book 135
　Appendix B: English Language Proficiency Tests ... 135
　Appendix C: Types of Placement Tests 135
　Appendix D: Tests and Testing 136
　Appendix E: Objective Tests 136
　Appendix F: Norm-Referenced Tests versus Criterion-Referenced Tests 136
　Appendix G: Testing 137
　Appendix H: Test Qualities 137
　Appendix I: Measurement and Evaluation 137
　Appendix J: The Test Development Process 138
　Appendix K: Classification of Tests 138
　Appendix L: Characteristics of a Good Test 138
　Appendix M: Early Work on Language Tests, Language Testing, and Language Proficiency 139

Abstract

The aim of this book is to investigate English tests used for multiple purposes globally. These language tests are used throughout the world to control the entry of students into university, predicting the ability of students to cope with English demands in university/college settings. They are also used as a part of border control processes. This book consists of five chapters, along with a summary and conclusion. Chapter one discusses the general concepts of language tests and language testing. Chapter two explains variable placement tests and placement testing. Chapter three focuses on test qualities, including reliability, validity, authenticity, interaction, impact, practicality, measurement and evaluation, assessment, and evaluation, and more. Chapter four reiterates the achievement tests which measure how much a language student has learned. It also measures students' aptitude for a second language or foreign language. Chapter five provides samples of language tests used for multiple purposes.

Preface

The significance of this book is embodied in the fact that language testing lags behind in the study of applied linguistics. Linguists advocate that tests should be used for screening purposes. Testing should apply to students and scholars who wish to partake in further studies that use foreign languages to deliver course content. In some countries in Africa and Asia, language testing of students to place them in appropriate course environments has, to date, been a neglected practice. Oversights in language testing study necessitated the publication of this book.

This book discusses the challenges of language testing that linguists need to work hard to overcome. It introduces language tests, language testing, English language proficiency assessments, and the use of such tests on an international scale. This book discusses other variable types of tests, including placement testing and language testing for specific purposes, and it outlines method testing, writing testing, grammar testing, vocabulary testing, reading comprehension testing, and oral ability testing. Test qualities and other types of tests used in language testing are also addressed.

Chapter One

Introduction

Many people find learning a foreign language difficult, sometimes feeling incapable of the task. Krashen (1992) proposes the theory that acquisition of language happens best when the learner's input contains forms and structures just beyond the learner's current competence in the language.

Hammad (2002) notes that, from distant history to the nineteenth century, there have been several attempts to create an artificial language to serve as a universal means of communication. The primary objective has been to construct a language that would bind the linguistically diverse peoples of the world into a connected whole.

In recent decades, English has begun to establish itself as this lingual centre, and many people have been deeply concerned by this prospect. As an imperial language, English appears to threaten the world's rich linguistic and cultural heritage. Linguistic rights activists have begun counteracting this universalising trend by implementing language repair and maintenance programs (Hammad, 2002). On the other hand, due to the current status of English as the global language of science, social science, technology, and international relations, many countries around the world consider the teaching of English a major educational priority (McKay, 2000).

Some linguists believe that language is a product of social processes and arises in the life of an individual through ongoing linguistic interactions with others. They argue that learning English as a second language or a foreign language is in the interest of social and political gain, giving English-as-a-second-language learners, speakers, and writers opportunities to succeed in school, university, and industry in a largely English-speaking world. Interest in learning English has increased drastically in recent years. English language education is now offered not only at post-secondary level but also in many high and junior school curriculums around the world.

This chapter will focus on the definitions of some keywords, language testing and its international uses, and English language proficiencies, beginning with proficiency tests.

1.1 Language, Performance, and Placement

1.1.1. Language
Warding and Ronald (1977) define language as a system of arbitrary focal symbols used for human communications.

1.1.2 Performance
Hubbard, Jones, Thomton, and Wheeler (1983) have devised a training course for testing English as a foreign language (TEFL) proficiency. They elucidate that performance of a language is defined as the actual utterances produced by the speakers of it.

1.1.3 Testing
Longman Dictionary of Applied Linguistics (1987) defines a test as a procedure for measuring ability, knowledge, or performance. Tests are used to compare individuals belonging to the same group.

1.1.4 Placement Testing

Morante (1986), an expert in language testing, defines placement testing as a term used in higher education to describe a process of student assessment, the results of which are used to place students in appropriate beginning courses. While processes of this nature have existed at many colleges for many years, proficiencies of entering students have declined over the past 20 years, increasing both the need for and the use of placement tests markedly.

1.1.5 Language Testing

Language testing has undergone a rapid evolution in the past 50 years, mirroring the development of applied linguistics more broadly (McNamara, 1991 p. 763). Language tests have great social relevance in the contemporary world, playing a role in socially significant institutional and political processes. The idea of formal tests of knowledge and ability first emerged in traditional China, where tests were used to identify and select individuals who would be trained to become members of the ruling elite. Tests, thus, played a crucial role in constructing the fundamental character of Chinese cultural and political life over many centuries (Fairbank & Goldman, 1998). In the modern world, language tests control access to international education by students studying in a second language—especially, but not exclusively, English—and they play an important role in the management of language education for the children of immigrants. Tests have been used as weapons in intergroup conflicts, acting as controls in the mobility of professionals and other workers. They are used for certifications of achievement, and in many countries, they control the transition between high schools and higher education, used to predict student ability to cope with the demands of university study.

Language tests have long been used as a form of border control, ever since the example of 'shibboleth' in the Bible (Judges 12:4-6). Soldiers trying to pass as members of the victorious ethnic group were quoted and slaughtered on the basis of minor discrepancies in their pronunciation of the /sh/ sound. Those trying to pass were required to say 'shibboleth' as a test of their pronunciation and, by extension, their identity. The use of language tests as part of a process of linguistic identification continues today.

Another recent example is a language test used to verify claims of German ethnicity. In the 1990s, people from minority German communities in Eastern Bloc countries wishing to immigrate to reunited Germany were expected to participate in an oral interview in German. The trained interviewers looked for evidence of non-standard forms of German in the speech of the interviewees. Non-standard German varieties indicated that the hopeful immigrants had learned German forms characteristic of German-speaking communities far removed from those of Germany proper.

The use of language tests as a form of border control is much more general than these examples suggest. In immigration contexts, language tests often feature as part of procedures used in controlling entry, with proficiency in the dominant language of the community immigrants aim to enter commonly used as a factor in considering requests for entry. It is argued that immigrants with local language proficiency are more likely to settle without difficulty and are less likely to require government services to assist in the acculturative process. For this reason, immigration applicants with high levels of proficiency in English and French are at an advantage in immigration selection procedures in Australia (Hawthorne, 1997; Ambrose, 2003). Similar applicant evaluation systems have recently been introduced for certain categories of immigrants, including highly skilled immigrants, in the United Kingdom (United Kingdom Home Office, 2002). Related issues have also been raised in Germany (Ruebec, 2002). The identity component of language proficiency tests of immigrants is clear in the inclusion of various forms of language tests in procedures for granting citizenship used in the United Kingdom and the United States. Germany recently introduced citizenship laws making it possible, for the first time, for people to acquire citizenship on the basis of residence, rather than blood, and it has included a language proficiency requirement as part of this evaluation. It is interesting that the most conservative states required to administer this law within Germany have been quick to seek the help of language testers to guide the required language tests, which are expected to stem the numbers of citizenship applicants (Rebelling, 2002).

The potential for the abuse of language tests in such contexts is most graphically illustrated in the case of the notorious Australian dictation test, which was used for about 30 years in early twentieth century as an instrument of blatant racial, political exclusion (Dutton, 1998; Jones, 1998; McNamara, 2001b). The test was adopted in the newly independent Australian federation of former British colonies from 1901 as a means of achieving the goals of the so-called White Australia Policy. People who arrived in Australia and were deemed undesirable on racial grounds were subjected to a dictation test of 100 words, which it was assumed they would fail to understand. Inevitably, the candidates failed the test, which was then used as grounds for exclusion; several thousand people were excluded from Australian entry. The dictation test was originally known as the education test and was based on a similar test implemented in the Natal colony in South Africa in the 1890s (Dutton, 1998).

Language testing is recognised institutionally within the applied linguistics discipline. It has its own journals and its own national and international conferences, and its own international professional association: the International Language Testing Association (ILTA).

Language testing is a subfield within applied linguistics. It has evolved and expanded in a number of ways over the last 20 years or so. At the first Language Testing Research Colloquium in 1979, the skills and the unitary hypothesis of language proficiency came under considerable criticism in light of a broadened view of language ability being espoused by proponents of communicative competence. In particular, the work of applied linguists such as Henry Widdoson (1978; 1979; 1983), Sandra Savignon (1972; 1983), Michael Canale, and Merrill Swain (1981) was to prove extremely influential on language testing in the decade to come.

1.2 Language Testing in China

In the west, language testing, while still emerging as a discipline in its own right, had established its status as a branch of applied linguistics throughout the 1990s (Bachman, 2000). In China, however, there was a delay of almost a decade, and it was not until the late 1990s that researchers really became interested in the development of valid and reliable measures for large numbers of test-takers, laying the foundations for language testing to emerge as an independent field in China's applied linguistics discipline. In recent years, with a growing number of tests, test-takers, practitioners, and researchers, the field of language testing has gained great momentum.

As a country where the history of imperial examinations dates back to the Sui dynasty (605 AD), China is known for its heavy reliance on testing for decision-making (Chieng, 2008; Jin, 2000; 2000b; Yang & Gui, 2007; Ziang, 2003). In present day China, research shows that the two most prominent English language tests currently are the National Matriculation English Test, taken by over 10 million high-school seniors each year, and the College English Test, taken by over 16 million college students each year. These exert a strong washback, both positive and negative, on English language education at secondary and tertiary levels (Gu, 2004; Jin, 2000; 2006a; 2006b; Qi, 2004; 2005).

Davies (1977) explains that language testing is both a social science and a practical activity and that it can have serious consequences, meaning that it should be based on a strong sense of professional morality, subject to codes, contracts, professional training, and ethical norms and standards; systematic attempts must be made to identify a professional ethos and to establish its norms.

Professionalisation of language testing has two major trusts: the training of testing professionals and the development of standards of practice, along with mechanisms for their implementation and enforcement. Language testing professionals now have more training resources, in the form of textbooks and course materials, than any other time in history. Well over dozens of textbooks for practitioners have been published in the past decade alone, and an entire new monograph series directed towards practitioners is set for publication with a major publisher (Alderson & Bachman, 2000).

Language testing, according to Johnson (2001, p. 187), involves many technologies and developments that are different from those used in language teaching, and yet language testing interacts closely with most aspects of language teaching. Gronlund (1985, p. 146) commented that the curation of good test items is an art form; a thorough grasp of subject matter, a clear concept of desired learning outcomes, a psychological understanding of pupils, a commitment to judgement persistence, and a touch of creativity are needed.

Jin (2010) designed a questionnaire to investigate the provision and instruction of language testing and assessment courses at tertiary level and to identify areas for improvement. The survey was designed to examine the backgrounds of instructors, teaching content and methodologies, teaching materials, and student perceptions of LTA courses provided as part of the curriculum of relevant programs for training future foreign language teachers. Hughes and Porter (1983), on the other hand, discussed three important developments in language testing. The first was a research program investigating the structure of foreign language ability. The second was the creation of reliable and valid measures of communicative competence. The third was the rise in the number of tests designed to test language proficiency for specific purposes, such as the study of engineering in Britain, as opposed to testing for general language ability. Hughes and Woods (1980) further investigated performance of 324 subjects representing linguistic geographic groups—Norway (108), Mexico (93), North Africa (53), and Hong

Kong (70)—on the Cambridge Proficiency Examination (CPE) in June 1980.

1.3. Proficiency

World-Class Instructional Design and Assessment, or WIDA (2004), says that proficiency is a step towards perfection—improvement in skills or knowledge. WIDA also calls proficiency a state or degree of improvement attained, a measure of adeptness and expertness.

1.3.1 Language Proficiency

Cummins (1983) comments that language proficiency cannot be conceptualised as one static entity. It is constantly developing through different dimensions—grammar, sociolinguistics, discourse, and strategic dimensions—and being specialised for different contexts of use among monolingual English-speaking, as well as language minority, children (Cummins, 1998, p.14).

1.3.2 English Language Proficiency and Academic English Language Proficiency

According to Cummins (1980), achieving English language proficiency is not a dichotomous process; it develops along a continuum. Social English proficiency (i.e. basic interpersonal conversational skills) takes an average of two to three years to develop, whereas academic English proficiency (i.e. cognitive academic language proficiency) takes an average of five to seven years to develop. Academic English proficiency has been found to be essential for educational contexts, though it can take significantly longer for students to develop the level of language proficiency needed for school success (Cummins, 1984). In addition to learning academic subjects in schools, English language learners are faced with English learning in other tasks and situations; this is referred to as the curriculum's double demand (Baker, Kameenui, & Simons, 1998; 2002; Gersten, 1999).

1.3.3 English Language Proficiency and its Relation to Academic English

Bachman and Winter (1986) demonstrate that traditional English Language proficiency tests may not consistently determine true proficiency or predict academic achievement because they each vary in their definitions of English proficiency. Duran (1988, p. 106) warns that language proficiency tests are intended to predict the ability to use language in criterion settings and are not intended to predict performance on criterion variables reflecting academic achievement or cognitive abilities divorced from language functioning. Duran suggests that English proficiency tests can provide information about the importance of considering language proficiency as a factor influencing the display of skills and aptitudes in non-native speakers.

1.3.4 Foreign Language Proficiency

According to Freed (1987), foreign language proficiency is defined by an ability to adapt to all language modalities—listening, writing, and speaking—and to assume the cultural framework of the language for the purpose of communicating ideas and information.

1.3.5 Foreign Language Proficiency Guidelines

Bachman and Savignon (1986) argue that guidelines that define language proficiency and its measurement could provide a basis for developing common metric tests for a wide range of language abilities in different contexts. Such tests would provide a standard for defining and measuring language proficiency that would be independent of specific languages, contexts, and domains of discourse; scores from these tests would be able to be applied comparatively across different languages and contexts. Guidelines would also provide a system for accountability in language teaching to students, administrators, taxpayers, parents, and potential future employers.

1.3.6 Communicative Language Proficiency

Bachman and Savignon (2011) state that the first systematic framework for describing the measurement of language proficiency was that incorporated in skills and component models such as those proposed in 1961 by Lado and

Caroll. These frameworks distinguished skills from components of knowledge—grammar, vocabulary, phonology—but did not indicate their relationships to each other.

On the other hand, Bachman and Palmer use the term 'communicative proficiency' to refer to language ability. For them, this includes language competencies, including grammatical, discourse, illocutionary and socio-linguistics, and skill modalities (reproductive visual).

Without adopting Bachman and Palmer's framework, the term 'communicative language proficiency' (CLP) retains the positive connotations of both communicative competence and proficiency.

1.4 English Language Proficiency Tests

The Longman Dictionary of Applied Linguistics (1985) describes English language proficiency tests as tests that can be based on the standard English vocabulary and grammar, regardless of English learning background.

1.4.1 IDEA Proficiency Test Results

The WIDA consortium (2004) explains the IDEA proficiency test as a test of English language proficiency designed to assess and categorise students on the basis of fluency in English speaking, reading, and writing. The IDEA proficiency test was originally developed in 1979 and was revised in 1991. Results are reported as three designations (six levels of oral language proficiency), and three of the levels are literacy. A post by No Child Left Behind, or NCLB, is currently used in Alaska and North Carolina.

1.4.2 Maculattis Assessment of Competencies Test of English Proficiency

In its second edition, the Maculattis-11 has the most grade-level cluster forms of the four ELP tests that measure oral language and literacy. Listening is assessed and reported independently from speaking. Five point rubrics are used to interpret oral language and writing samples. Results are then distributed into five levels of literacy. A post NCLB revised MAC-11 is currently being used in Missouri.

1.4.3 Stanford English Language Proficiency

The Stanford English Language Proficiency Test, or SELPT, is the most recent commercially designed English language proficiency instrument and was designed following the passage of NCLB. The Stanford English Language Proficiency Test provides results for listening, writing, reading, and speaking proficiency, with student performance being classified at emergent, basic, intermediate, or proficient levels. This test is currently being used in Mississippi and Virginia. MAC-II and SELPT were both designed by WIDA (2004), together with the IDEA Proficiency Test.

Chapter Two
Variable Placement Tests

2.1 Placement Testing

According to Green and Weir (2004), placement testing is an area that has received comparatively little attention in language testing research. Books on practical aspects of testing (Harrison, 1983; Hughes 1990; Bachman, 1990; Heaton, 1990; Anderson et al., 1995; Bachman & Palmer, 1996; Brown, 1996) outline two fundamental roles for placement tests: to aid the creation of student groups of homogeneous language ability and to probe students' mastery of course content.

Usually, one of these roles dominates as a result of practical considerations, such as the diversity of students, the flexibility of administrators, and the cost-effectiveness of test implementation, along with the educational need for homogeneous ability groups (Bachman, 1990; Brown, 1996). Wesche et al. (1996) suggest that resource deficits place constraints on testing practices in most settings. Nevertheless, several authors have discussed the potential for placement test results to inform teaching and contribute to the evaluation of instructional programs.

2.2 Global Placement Test

Green and Weir (2004) also discuss the Global Placement Test, arguing that studies of placement tests are typically narrowly concerned with validation as instruments for efficient grouping of students. They rarely explore assumptions that placement content can be related to classroom tasks, thus informing instructional decisions. Green and Weir argue that the Global Placement Test offers a more effective, universalised approach to measuring grammatical knowledge and is developed for use in language schools worldwide. Green and Weir's central concern is the extent to which the Global Placement Test can enable schools to make valid inferences and assumptions about student mastery of grammatical structures to be taught in relevant courses. They say that the Global Placement Test is designed to measure knowledge of grammatical items expressing temporal relations in English and was administered to 1,070 EFL (English as a foreign language) learners studying in the United Kingdom, Greece, and Japan. That dimensionality of the Global Placement Test as a measure was investigated by item response theory (IRT) and factor analytic methods. The analysis suggests that item difficulty is affected by an inherent linguistic difficulty of the element of grammatical competence being tested.

2.3 Placement Tests as Adaptive Tests

WIDA (2006) describes the placement test as an adaptive test that can gauge students' proficiency up to and beyond level 5 of the WIDA English language proficiency standards. Like ACCESS for English language learners, there are five grade-level clusters (kindergarten, 1-2, 3-5, 6-8, and 9-12). Unlike ACCESS for English language learners, all scoring of the WIDA-Adaptive Placement Test is completed on site by a test administrator. All sections of the test are scored as the test is administered. After completion of the speaking, listening, reading, and writing examinations, the test administrator uses the instructions on the scoring sheet to calculate the overall proficiency levels of participating students.

2.4 Placement Testing as an Essential Ingredient

Morante (1987) claims that placement testing is an essential ingredient of a successful college program. Students bring diverse backgrounds and levels of proficiency to colleges, and this variation demands individualised attention and course selection processes. To place all students in the same level of course is to significantly increase the probability of lowering standards or failing large numbers of students. Placement tests and their subsequent scores play important roles in access, retention, and quality of education. Colleges need to place as much emphasis on the careful selection of appropriate placement tests as they do on curriculum development and student recruitment. Any college that does not recognise this interaction will pay a high price, as will its students.

2.5 Who Should Be Tested?

Morante (1986) also poses a question: Who should be tested for language proficiency? He answers by saying that all entering students who need or who will be helped by a course or by a level of a course outside the regular college-level program should be tested for language proficiency. A placement test, or a battery of tests, is essential in determining which courses or which levels of courses are most appropriate for individual students. Used in conjunction with other background information, test scores are fundamental tools in appropriate course placement. Individualised course placement is an important step in retaining students.

2.6 Placement Test Selection

Morante (1987) also reiterates the importance of appropriate selection of a placement test. He says that an appropriate placement test is one of the most important factors in creating a comprehensive developmental education program. Placement tests and cut scores that are used cannot be differentiated from the standards of quality set by colleges. Nine factors should be considered in any decision about a particular placement test, including an in-house test: the test content, referencing, discrimination, speediness, reliability, validity, cost, control for guessing, and the availability of alternate forms.

2.7 Test and Testing
2.7.1 Tests

Caroll (1968) provides the following definition of a test: 'A psychological or educational test is a procedure designed to elicit certain behaviour from which one can make inferences about certain characteristics of an individual.' From this definition, it follows that a test is a measurement instrument designed to elicit a specific sample of an individual's behaviour. As one type of measurement, a test necessarily quantifies characteristics of an individual according to explicit procedures. What distinguishes a test from other types of measurements is that it is designed to obtain a specific sample of behaviour. Consider the following: The Interagency Language Round Table (ILT) Oral Interview (Lowe, 1982) is a speaking test consisting of a set of elicitation procedures, including a sequence of activities and set of question types and topics. It operates using a measurement scale of language proficiency, ranging from a low level 0 to level 5, by which samples of oral language obtained via elicitation procedures are rated.

Razaq (2005) discusses what tests measure. Examination, he says, is used to refer to a set of longer subjective questions. He explains that testing is very important. Good tests help to promote positive student attitudes and can support students in mastering the language, providing opportunities to foster learning through diagnostic characteristics. Furthermore, Razaq elucidates that tests can sustain or enhance class morale and learning. They are produced as teaching devices, as well as being natural steps in the educational process. They act as guides to both students and teachers (Rivers, 1968).

2.7.2 Tests and Examinations

Pilliner (1968) explains that tests, like examinations, invite candidates to display their knowledge or skills in a concentrated fashion, enabling the results to be graded and inferences to be made from the standard of performance displayed in the test about the general standard of performance that can be expected from the tested candidates. Pilliner goes further, stating that the difference between tests and examinations lies in the marking. The marking of an examination requires the use of judgement, whereas the marking of a test is not dependent on any individual. A test is a measuring device used to compare an individual to other individuals who belong to the same group.

Pilliner (1976) also reveals that a loose definition is often made to distinguish between examinations and tests. Since both give rise to many testers, the desirable quality measures of attribute possessed by an individual and the distinction in terms of outcome are difficult to justify. Sometimes, the distinction is made in terms of time allowed; a typical examination lasts for two or more hours, while a typical test last between half an hour and an hour. From this, it has become common to call a group of tests all administered to the same participants an examination. The distinction may also be hierarchical. A university professor examines his final honours students in English literature, while a primary school teacher tests her nine-year-old students in spelling. Finally, the distinction may be made based on whether assessment is subjective or objective. Subjective assessments are typically referred to as examinations, while objective assessments are typically referred to as tests. There is no single conventional distinction that is universally accepted, but the last mentioned will be adopted. Subjective examining instruments will be called examinations, and their counterparts will be called tests.

2.7.3 Direct and Indirect Tests

Bachman and Savignon (2011) explain that the term 'direct test' is often used to refer to a test in which performance resembles actual or normal language performance, while an indirect test is one in which performance is perceived as somehow different from the actual or normal. Thus, writing samples and oral interviews are referred to as direct tests because they involve the use of the skills being tested. By extension, such tests are often regarded, virtually without question, as valid measures of language abilities.

2.7.4 Subjective and Objective Tests

Pilliner (1976) discusses two contrasting testing procedures.

The first procedure is a subjective test, a test in which the examinee answers, in his own words and at appropriate length, all or some of a relatively small number of questions. Typical keywords in the questions set in examinations of this kind are 'discuss,' 'compare,' 'contrast,' and 'describe.' The answers they elicit are often essays, ranging in length from a single sentence to a dozen or more paragraphs. Assessment of examinee performance is subjective in the sense that its merit must be evaluated or judged by an examiner. Two examples of essay type questions are (a)

'Discuss Shakespeare's sonnets' and (b) 'Who said the following and to what end? (Answer in no more than two sentences).'

The second procedure is an objective test, in which the examinee responds to each of a large number of questions by selecting one or more of several answer options provided with questions, supplying a single word or otherwise indicating their knowledge or lack thereof. These answers are commonly called responses. Assessment of the merit of the examinee's work is objective in the sense that no evaluative judgement is needed on the part of the examiner.

2.7.5 Tests and Quizzes

Both tests and quizzes play a role in the foreign language classroom. The distinction between tests and quizzes is one of dimensions and purposes, rather than item content (Lado, 1965). A test is announced in advance and covers a specific unit of instruction. Classroom tests may be given every two or three weeks, in some cases every week. Such tests may be constructed to last the entire class period; in this case, optimum learning efficiency requires teachers to return and discuss the corrected test as soon as the class meets again.

Conversely, the essence of a quiz is brevity. Quizzes may be administered unannounced, so frequent quizzes encourage students to devote time regularly to their language study. Moreover, quizzes enable teachers to acquaint students with the types of items that might subsequently be used in tests. The spontaneous nature of quizzes reduces the negative impacts of nervousness on performance (Valetta, 1967).

2.7.6 Oral and Written Tests

Language involves speaking and writing. The form of a test depends on which skill is being assessed. If the goal is to test the learner's knowledge of the orthographic system, written tests should be used. If the goal is to measure knowledge of phonology, spoken tests are preferable. Generally speaking, it is through the written form that all aspects of grammatical competence except phonological knowledge are assessed.

2.7.6.1 Oral Tests

Oral tests usually take the form of an interview or conversation between a student and a teacher. There are two types of oral tests. First, short answer oral tests include transformations, such as changing sentences from one tense to another, changing the active voice into passive while answering questions about a topic chosen by the teacher, and reading passages from textbooks. Second, oral composition tests include describing pictures of places or objects, telling stories, or making a point related to a predetermined subject.

2.7.6.2 Written Tests

Written tests can take one or more of the following forms: written composition on a subject assigned by the teacher, guided or free; dictation, mainly used to test spelling; objective written tests, which are of various types; and vocabulary tests, which assess the appropriate use of words in sentences.

2.7.7 Objective Tests

Objective tests take the form of one of the following: true or false tests, multiple-choice tests, or matching tests.

2.7.8 True or False Tests

True or false tests involve the acceptance or rejection of a statement or utterance heard or read. They are most useful as tests of listening or reading comprehension or of knowledge of historical, literary, or cultural facts related to foreign language study. These tests have been criticised because their two-way nature makes the probability of success in guessing much higher than in other forms of tests, like multiple-choice tests.

2.7.9 Multiple-Choice Tests

Multiple-choice tests provide answers to questions on, for example, listening or reading comprehension material, lexical meanings of words, and appropriateness of rejoinder in spoken language. Of the answers supplied, only one is correct, the other options often based on likely errors in vocabulary misinterpretation, structural relationships in reading comprehension, and similar words or phrases.

2.7.10 Matching Tests

Matching tests are commonly used as vocabulary tests. Students are asked to match synonyms, antonyms, names of objects, and so on.

2.7.11 Norm-Referenced Tests versus Criterion-Referenced Tests

2.7.11.1 Norm-Referenced Test

Norm-referenced tests measure how students perform in comparison to the performance of their peers. When administered on a large scale using accepted statistical procedures, these types of tests are often referred to as standardised. Results are given in terms of percentile.

2.7.11.2 Criterion-Referenced Test

Criterion-referenced tests measure how well students meet specific objectives. A driver's license test is an example of a criterion-referenced test; test-takers either achieve a pass or a fail, the outcome being determined according to a clear set of criteria.

2.7.12 Indirect Tests versus Direct Tests

Indirect tests do not examine students' ability to perform in authentic situations. For example, a test of lexical items relating to history might be used to predict how well students will be able to function in a history class with native speakers of their target language. Most will agree that such a test would probably not be a very good predictor in this situation. Indirect tests do not test actual performance. Rather, they test enabling skills or micro-skills, which are supposed to add up to what might constitute actual performance.

Direct tests are usually much closer to testing abilities and thus yield more accurate results. For example, tests that assess the ability to gather important ideas from a lecture, to write a summary or an essay expressing an opinion, and to read and understand academic written discourse provide a relatively comprehensive indication of expected student performance.

Performance tasks might be used in such testing to improve authenticity.

2.7.13 Discrete Point Tests versus Integrative Tests

No less important than the distinctions mentioned above is the discrete point test versus the integrative test distinction. This distinction has profound implications, not only for testing in second and foreign languages but for teaching them as well.

Discrete point tests emerged from a behaviourist/structural approach to language learning and teaching, in which contrastive analysis was the main focus. Discrete point tests examine knowledge of specific elements of phonology, grammar, and vocabulary in order to determine proficiency in isolated skill areas of listening, reading, speaking, and writing. These assessments determine whether students can aurally distinguish between similar-sounding words, recognise tense forms, and comprehend vocabulary words.

Integrative tests, on the other hand, emerged from a communicative approach to language learning and teaching. Integrative tests examine students' ability to use many skills simultaneously when accomplishing a task. Students are assessed on their ability to answer typical conversational questions, determine the meanings of selected passages, tell comprehensible stories, and write an effective letter.

2.8 Testing

2.8.1 Testing Language for Specific Purposes

Early work on testing language for specific purposes (LSP) inspired a growth in the movement towards teaching LSP (Morrow, 1977; Caroll, 1981; Weir, 1983). LSP testing was informed largely by developments in specification of syllabi, particularly the communicative framework of Munby (1978). For an interview on English for specific purposes (ESP), see Clapham (1996); for an interview on LSP, see Douglas (1997).

The past decade has seen an expansion of activity in this area, much of it centred around the design and development of the English Language Testing Service, now the International English Language Testing System (IELTS), which was the largest experiment to date in standardised large-scale LSP testing (Alderson & Clapham, 1996).

2.8.2 Testing Methods

Pilliner (1968), in discussing testing methods, reveals that one of the important characteristics to be considered in describing a test is the specific testing method used. Given the variety of methods that have been devised and continue to be devised, together with the creativity of test developers, it is not possible to make an exhaustive list of the methods used for language tests.

One broad type of method that has been discussed widely by language testers is the performance test, in which the test-takers' performance is expected to replicate their language performance in non-test situations (Jones 1985a, 1985b; Wesche, 1985). The oral interview and the essay are considered examples of performance tests. However, multiple-choice, dictation, and cloze point tests are not themselves single methods; they consist of different combinations of features, instruction input types, and task types. Test method facets such as these provide more precise ways of describing and distinguishing different types than single category labels.

2.8.3 Testing Grammar

Hughes (2004) and Lado (1968) argue that, even if one has doubt about testing grammar in proficiency tests, there is often good cause to include a grammar component in achievement, placement, and diagnostic tests of teaching institutions. Whether or not grammar has an important place in an institution's teaching, it must be accepted that grammatical ability, or lack thereof, sets limit to what can be achieved in the way of language skills performance. The successful achievement of academic assignments, for example, must depend, to some extent, on command of more than the most elementary grammatical structures. From this, it follows that, in order to place students in the most appropriate classes for the development of such skills, knowledge of a student's grammatical ability is very useful information.

Hughes further argues that most proficiency tests that are administered on a large scale retain a grammar element. Testing grammar, vocabulary, reading comprehension, oral ability, and writing is of great importance in proficiency and placement testing. The specifications of a placement test usually include all of the structures taught in the syllabus. Proficiency and diagnostic tests based on a national-functional approach are especially useful.

2.8.4 Testing Vocabulary

According to Lado (1968), vocabulary tests have been prepared as measures of general ability or intelligence and of achievement in special subject fields. Frequency of occurrence of words has been counted in large samples of up to five million words for English by E.L Thorndike. Frequency of various meanings of words have been counted for English also by

Lorge and Thorndike. Limited vocabularies have been prepared for students of English, Spanish, Russian, French, German, and Portuguese. When testing vocabulary, we are interested in lexical units. Languages use words as the chief linguistic forms for lexical units, and all these lexical units are words.

2.8.5 Testing Reading Comprehension

Lado (1965) says that reading in a foreign language consists of grasping meaning in that language through its written representation. Furthermore, he explains that the general technique for testing reading comprehension in a foreign language consists of presenting students with passages containing reading problems and assessing comprehension of the passage at the points at which the problems occur. He continued, stating that, for students for whom graphic representation will be a significant learning problem, tests may need to be implemented to assess identification of graphic symbols without going through the full process of reading.

On the other hand, Hughes (2004) claims that testing reading ability seems deceptively straightforward when it is compared to, say, the testing of oral ability. You take a passage, ask some questions about it, and there you are. But while it is true that one can very quickly construct a reading test, it may not be a very good test, and it may not measure its subject in accurate, specific ways. The problem is that the exercise of receptive skills does not necessarily, or usually, manifest itself directly in behaviour. When students write and speak, assessors see and hear; when students read and listen, there is often nothing to observe. The challenge for language testers is to set tasks that not only cause students to exercise reading skills but result in behaviour that effectively demonstrates the successful use of these skills.

2.8.6 Testing Oral Ability

Hughes (2004) says that the development of spoken language skills is integral to the development of the ability to interact successfully in that language, and this involves both comprehension and production.

According to Hughes, the basic problem in testing oral ability is essentially the same as that in writing testing. Thus, we must set tasks that form a representative sample of the population of oral tasks that students are expected to be able to perform; the tasks should elicit behaviour that truly represents the candidates' ability, and the samples of behaviour should be scored validly and reliably.

Hughes further points out that the most common format for testing oral interaction is the interview. Yes/no questions should generally be avoided unless they are asked at the beginning of the interview, while the candidate is still warming up. Tests must be planned carefully and should follow some pattern. Hughes believes that it is a mistake to begin an interview with no more than a general idea of the course it might take. Hughes also advocates testing processes that require candidates to interact with more than one tester.

In connection with oral testing, Davies (1976) presented an oral English test, employed by the West African Examination Council, called the McCallien Test. The McCallien Test has been in use for some 10 to 12 years. The four West African countries that used the McCallien Test were Ghana, Sierra Lieone, Gambia, and Nigeria. Students who sat the test and passed successfully were awarded a general certificate of English (GCE).

The McCallien Test (May 1965 version) comprised:

(a) Production of English by Reading Test

(i) Students have 10 minutes to prepare to read a passage of about 150 words, which they then read aloud to the examiner twice and are assessed for production of segmental phonemes (20 items).

(ii) In a production of stress and non-stress test, students prepare short sentences to be read aloud (10 items).

(iii) Students complete an intonation and emphasis test (10 minutes).

(b) Comprehension

(i) The examiner reads a word containing a potential phonemic contrast and asks students to make up a sentence containing that word and those phonemes (2 items).

(ii) The examiner reads a word containing a potential phonemic contrast as in (i) above and asks students to spell it.

(c) Conversation

The examiner engages students in three to five minutes of conversation, in which credit is given for fluency, intelligibility, vocabulary, and the use of idiomatic forms.

2.8.7 Testing Writing

Lado (1965) elucidates that writing fluently in a foreign language is defined as the ability to use the language and its graphic representation in ordinary writing situations. More specifically, writing in a foreign language requires the ability to use the structures, lexical items, and conventional representations of that language in ordinary matter of writing.

Chapter Three
3.1 Test Qualities

For many testers, the desirable qualities of a test include validity, reliability, and practicality (Hughes, 2003, p. 56). Different authors include various aspects under the heading of validity, including construct, face, and content validity, criterion-based and scoring validity, and concurrent and predictive validity (Hughes, 2003, p. 26-33). Bachman and Palmer (1996, p. 17-18) propose a model of test usefulness based on six qualities of tests:

1. Reliability

Reliability is the 'consistency of scores from one set of tests and test tasks to another' (Bachman & Palmer, 1996, p. 19-20). It can be assessed by means of various statistical analyses, including split-half reliability or Kuder Richardson (KR) 20 and 21 inches, parallel-form, and test-retest methods (Alderson et al., 1995, p. 87-89).

2. Construct Validity

Construct validity refers to the extent to which a given test score can be interpreted as an indicator of the ability or construct it aims to measure (Bachman & Palmer, 1996, p. 21). To achieve this, the construct must be defined as closely and clearly as possible.

3. Authenticity

Authenticity 'relates the test task to the domain of generalisation to which we want our score interpretations to generalise' (Bachman & Palmer, 1996, p. 23-24).

4. Interactiveness

Interactiveness can be described as how a test task engages the test-taker's language knowledge, meta-cognitive strategies, topical knowledge, and affective scheme and is dependent on the interaction between the test-taker and the task.

5. Impact

Impact relates to the fact that tests are virtually always designed and implemented to serve the needs of an educational system or society at large (Bachman, 1990). Bachman and Palmer (1996, p. 29-30) describe the relationship between test-taking and the use of test scores and the micro-level (affecting individuals) of education systems.

6. Practicality

Practicality is slightly different to the other qualities as it relates to the implementation of the test and whether it will be developed and used, rather than how the test scores will be used. To assess the practicality of a test, the resources required must be defined and divided by the resources available. If the result is equal to or greater than one, the test is deemed practical, but if it is not, a reallocation of or an increase in resources is necessary (Bachman & Palmer, 1995, p. 35).

Hughes (2005, p. 8-9) relates judgement to reliability and validity. She argues that the purpose of testing is to measure language proficiency, discover how successful students have achieved objectives in a course of study, diagnose students' strengths and weaknesses, and assist placement of students by identifying the stage or level of teaching program most appropriate to their ability.

3.2 Measurement and Evaluation

Bachman (1990, p. 19-23) says that the terms 'measurement' and 'evaluation' are often used synonymously. Indeed, they may, in practice, refer to the same activity. When we ask for an evaluation of an individual's language proficiency, for example, we are frequently given a test score. This attention to the superficial similarities between these two terms, however, tends to obscure the distinctive characteristics of each. Bachman believes that an understanding of the distinctions between the terms is vital to the proper development and use of language tests.

3.2.1 Measurement

According to Bachman (1990), measurement in the social sciences is the process of quantifying characteristics of persons according to explicit procedures and rules.

3.2.2 Evaluation

Weiss (1972) calls evaluation a systematic gathering of information for the purpose of making decisions. The probability of making a correct decision in any given situation is a function not only of the ability of the decision maker but also of the quality of information upon which the decision is based. Everything else being equal, the more reliable and relevant the information, the better the likelihood of making the correct decision. On the other hand, tests are often used as a means of motivating students to study or as a means of reviewing material taught, in which cases no evaluative decision is made on the basis of the test results. Tests may also be used for purely descriptive purposes. It is only when the results of tests are used as a basis for decision-making that evaluation is involved.

3.3 Testing and Evaluation

According to Omran (2006), testing is an essential component of educational evaluation. This evaluation is instrumental in determining what is to be taught and learnt. Educators set objectives first. Then follows the teaching and learning experience, and finally, the development of evaluation procedures, which are, in turn, based on the teaching-learning experience and the objectives.

Tests are monitors of teaching and learning. The materials of teaching are not the only factors that contribute to the effectiveness of language learning. The teacher and the learner are important factors as well. However, only teaching materials act as controls, and they happen to be the items in which the applied linguist is chiefly concerned. Tests are not an end in themselves. They are closely linked to the process of measurement and evaluation. Measuring the learner's knowledge is a means of evaluating not only the learner himself but also the teacher and teaching materials.

3.4 Assessment and Evaluation
3.4.1 Assessment

Hutchinson and Waters (1987, p. 19) state that assessment is a measurement of the ability of a person or the quality or success of a teaching course. Assessment may be conducted by test interview or observation.

For instance, assessment of the comprehension of an immigrant child may be necessary to determine whether the child will be able to follow a course of study at school or whether extra language teaching is needed. A student may be tested at the beginning and again at the end of the course of study to measure improvement (Richards, Platt, & Webber, 1985).

3.4.2 Evaluation

Evaluation uses both quantitative methods (tests) and qualitative methods (observations), the latter including rating and value judgements. In language planning, evaluation frequently involves gathering information on patterns of language teaching programs. Evaluation results are related to decisions about individuals in the programs being examined. The evaluation of a teaching program may include the study of curriculum, objectives, and materials and a test on grading systems. The evaluation of individuals involves decisions about entrance to programs and individual tests. Other measurements are frequently used (Richards, Platt, & Webber, 1985).

3.5 The Test Development Process

Various authors have proposed different stages in test development. Bachman and Palmer (1996, p. 86) propose a three-stage test development process involving design, operationalisation, and administration.

3.5.1 Design

The test design process involves describing the components of the test that enable test tasks to reflect target language use as closely as possible in order to achieve maximum usefulness of test scores. A design statement is developed, describing the purposes of the test, the task types, test-taker characteristics, the constructs of the task-takers, the evaluation of the test as well as the resources required.

3.5.2 Operationalisation

At this stage, test task specification and a blueprint for the test tasks, rubrics, and scoring procedures are written (Bachman & Palmer, 1996, p. 90).

3.5.3 Administration

The test is administered, and information is collected to analyse the usefulness of the test and to make the decisions that the test was intended to inform (Bachman & Palmer, 1996, p. 91).

3.6 Modern Trends in Language Testing

In order to come to a decision about the form included in any test/examination, test curators and administrators must be aware of the various approaches of language testing concerned with validity, reliability, and efficiency. Validity is concerned with the degree to which a test measures what it is supposed to measure. Reliability is concerned with the extent to which the results can be relied upon. Efficiency deals with the application and cost of designing and administering the test.

Davies (1978) says that even in the 1970s, the approaches of testing ranged from discrete point tests to integrative tests as cloze tests. He believes that the best way to design tests is to mix the two approaches. The two poles—the discrete point tests and integrative tests—are similar and can be connected with the validity and reliability concept (Davies, 1998, p. 20).

3.7 Uses of Language Tests in Educational Programs

Bachman (1990 p. 54-55) says that the most important feature in both the development of language tests and the representation of their results is the purpose or purposes that they are intended to serve. According to Bachman, the two major uses of language tests are as sources of information for making decisions within the context of educational programs and as indicators of abilities or attributes that are of interest in research or language acquisition and language teaching. In educational settings, the major uses of test scores are related to evaluation, decision-making, and programs. In order to justify the use of tests for educational evaluation, certain assumptions and considerations must be made regarding the usefulness and quality of information tests provide. An understanding of these assumptions and considerations, as well as of different types of appropriate use of language tests and the roles of these types in evaluation, is essential to the appropriate use of language tests.

Bachman continued, stating that the fundamental uses of language testing in educational programs is to provide information for decision-making processes—that is, for evaluation. An educational program, in the broadest sense, is any situation in which one or more persons are engaged in teaching and learning. Educational programs, therefore, range in scope from individual tutoring, to school, to nationwide programs. Evaluation, on the other hand, comprises essentially of two components: information and value judgements or decisions. The information relevant to evaluation can be either qualitative or quantitative.

3.8 Classification of Tests

Venkates Waran (1950) classifies tests into the following categories:

1. Knowledge tests, as contrasted with performance or skill tests

2. Subjective and objective tests

3. Productive and receptive tests

4. Language sub-skill tests and communication skill tests

5. Norm-referenced tests and criterion-referenced tests

6. Discrete point tests and integrative tests

7. Proficiency tests and achievement tests

8. Speed tests

3.9 Characteristics of a Good Test

According to Omran (2005), a test is a tool by which we measure the achievement of our pupils. Like any other tool, tests can be exciting or dull, useful or useless. The following are among the features regarded as characteristics of a useful language test:

3.9.1 Validity

Corder distinguishes three types of validity. Validity refers to the degree to which a test measures what it is supposed to measure or can be used successfully for the purposes for which it is intended. A number of different statistical procedures generally seek to determine what a test measures and how well it does so. That is, in order to be a good test, the test must produce scores that are valid.

(a) Content Validity

Learners are required to perform the activities that they have been taught to perform over the course of their study. Establishing content validity, unlike establishing predictive and concurrent validity, does not involve comparison with results of other tests. It is, therefore, a matter of expert judgement and is, to some extent, subjective and unreliable.

(b) Predictive Validity

Predictive validity is a validity used to predict the success of learners in tasks, such as studying language at a university, depending on their knowledge of their target language.

(c) Concurrent Validity

When the results of a test are confirmed by other tests aiming to measure the same thing, validity is established. Rivers considers validity in foreign language tests unattainable without a great deal of thought and analysis before the test is constructed.

3.9.2 Reliability

A good test must be reliable. In language testing, we seek to achieve reliability through objectivity, but the objectivity of the examiner or observer is not enough. Testing requires sampling, but sampling is not always reliable in and of itself. Lado suggests that sampling should concentrate on points that are difficult for learners and that these can be discovered through differences between the mother tongue and the target language. It has been stated that we do not, as yet, have any satisfactory and comprehensive accounts of differences between languages and that these differences do not always mean difficulties. A test may be unreliable for reasons other than those connected with sampling. A syntactic test item may contain vocabulary the learner does not know. The instructions may be vitiated by the learner's inadequate performance ability. To overcome these difficulties, the test materials are carefully revised to eliminate any items that may produce erratic results. This process is known as item analysis.

3.9.3 Discrimination

Many classroom tests are constructed to assess the extent to which a class as a whole has mastered a particular syllabus. However, most other tests are designed to show the differences in the performances of individual test-takers, thus aiming to differentiate as widely as possible between test-takers.

3.9.4 Backwash

The term 'backwash,' or 'washback,' as it is sometimes referred to, refers to the effects of tests on teaching. A good backwash has a good influence on learning and teaching. A good test or an examination must be neither too demanding nor too easy for those taking it. It must measure and be proved to measure the specific ability or knowledge it is intended to measure, and it must be capable of producing answers that can be accurately marked so that any examiner will award the same mark to the same piece of work.

3.9.5 Objectivity

If two or more independent people score one paper or one set of papers, they must award the same number of marks, marking by objective means. Tests constructed in such a way leave no room for the subjective opinions or biases of examiners.

3.9.6 Scorability

Each section of a test is attributed a definite and agreed upon mark, which is distributed among the subsections either evenly or according to level of importance. In scoring composition tests, it has been useful both for subjectivity and scorability to point out in advance the types of competence examinees are expected to display and to outline all of the specific marks for each type.

3.9.7 Practicability

Tests should always be practicable, meaning that they can be administered. Often, oral tests cannot be completed when teachers are short of time. Some tests are expensive or too long for learners. Such tests are impracticable.

Wilga Rivers offers guidelines for the construction of a useful test. She says that tests should be conceived as teaching devices and natural steps in the educational process. They should serve a two-fold instructional purpose, acting as a guide to the student and as a guide to the teacher. According to Rivers, to construct a good and useful test, teachers should know what they are intending to test, choose to test just one thing at a time, distinguish the various aspects of performance, test only what has been taught, and test to find out what students know. Questions are often framed in such a way that successful students are those who are best able to interpret their teachers' intentions.

The researcher agrees with Rivers; from a practical point of view, a teacher who is designing class tests should ask him or herself the following questions:

1 Are the instructions in the test so clear that no student can misunderstand what he or she is expected to do?

2 Is there any ambiguity in the test items? No item should be included that allows several possible answers unless it is clear to the student that all of these answers will be acceptable.

3 Is the test constructed so that the student begins with easier items and proceeds to the more difficult? If difficult questions are placed early in the test, weaker students may become anxious and find it difficult to answer even the easier questions.

4 Do the items test the students' ability to use the language, as opposed to merely testing knowledge about the language? According to modern methods of teaching, language is taught through use. Students must not be expected to make formal statements about language structure; formal descriptions of the way a language functions should be expected only of students who are undertaking advanced studies at university level.

5 Are the items in the test linguistically useful? Test items should concentrate on normal usage, not on unusual forms. Items should consist of complete utterances unless there are valid reasons for using segments of utterances.

Chapter Four
Other Variable Types of Tests Used in Language Testing

4.1 Achievement Tests

Achievement tests measure how much of a language student have learned with reference to a particular course of study or program of instruction. The difference between achievement tests and more general proficiency tests is that the latter are not linked to any particular course of instruction. For example, an achievement test might be a listening comprehension test based on a particular set of dialogues that appear in a textbook. The test helps the teacher to judge the success of his or her teaching and to identify the common weaknesses of students. A proficiency test might use similar items, but it is not linked to any particular textbook or language syllabus. Language achievement tests and language proficiency tests differ mainly in the way they are prepared and interpreted (Vallette, 1977).

4.2 Language Aptitude Tests

Language aptitude tests measure students' aptitude for second language or foreign language learning and can be used to identify learners who are most likely to succeed. Language aptitude tests usually consist of several different test measuring abilities, such as:

(a) Sounding ability: the ability to identify and remember new sounds in a foreign or second language.

(b) Grammatical coding ability: the ability to identify the grammatical functions of different parts of sentences.

(c) Inductive learning ability: the ability to work out meanings without explanation in a new language.

(d) Memorisation: the ability to remember words, rules, and so on in a new language.

(Vallette, 1977, p. 155).

4.3 Diagnostic Tests

Diagnostic tests are designed to show what skills or knowledge learners know and don't know. For example, a diagnostic pronunciation test may be used to measure a learner's pronunciation of English sounds, showing which sounds the student is and is not able to pronounce. Diagnostic tests can be used to find out how much a learner already knows prior to engaging with a language course (Vallette, 1977, p. 80).

4.4 Progress Tests

Most classroom tests take the form of progress tests, which assess the progress of students by measuring material taught in the class syllabus. These tests also enable students to assess the success of teaching and learning and to identify areas of weakness and difficulty. Progress tests can also be diagnostic to some degree.

4.5 Formative Tests

Formative tests are administered during a course of instruction and inform both students and teachers of how well students are doing. Formative tests include only topics that have been taught in class and show whether students need extra work or attention in particular areas of study. These tests are usually pass or fail. If a student fails, he or she is generally able to do more study and take test again.

4.6 Summative Tests
Summative tests are given at the end of a course of instruction, working to measure or sum up how much a student has learned from a course. Summative tests are usually graded tests, meaning that they are marked according to a scale or set of grades (Vallette, 1977).

4.7 Essay Tests
Essay tests are subjective tests in which students are required to write an extended piece of text on a set topic.

4.8 Hypothesis Tests
In language learning, hypothesis tests examine students' ideas about a language to see whether they are right or wrong. The most obvious way of doing this is to use a hypothesis to produce

new utterances and see whether they work. But one can also compare one's own utterances with those of other people speaking the language or imagine what other people would say in a particular situation, then see whether they do typically say it. Scholars who hold the innatist hypothesis have claimed, in effect, that the number of hypotheses about a new language that need to be tested is finite. Some hypotheses are simply never formed because of knowledge of language universals present in every normal human at birth (Vallette, 1977p. 133).

4.9 Subtests
Subtests are given as part of longer tests. For example, a language proficiency test may contain subtests of grammar, writing, speaking, reading, listening, oracy, and so on.

4.10 Test-Retest Reliability
Test-retest reliability is an estimate of the reliability of a test determined by the extent to which a test gives the same results if it is

administered at two different times. Reliability is estimated from the coefficient of a correlation, which is obtained from the two administrations of the test.

4.11 TOEFL Tests

TOEFL tests are tests of English as a foreign language. They are standardised tests of English proficiency administered by the Educational Testing Service, and they are widely used to measure the English language proficiency of foreign students wishing to enter American universities.

4.12 Problems in Language Testing

4.12.1 Problem 1

Morante (1987) states that the problems encountered in language testing include the costs of materials, administration, and scoring.

4.12.2 Problem 2

Bachman (1990), Brown (1996), and Wesche (1996) argue that resource deficits jeopardise or constrain testing practices in most settings to such an extent that fundamental roles for variable tests, such as to aid the creation of student groups of homogeneous language ability and to probe students' mastery of course content, cannot be adequately addressed.

4.12.3 Problem 3

Davies (1997) argues that there are two problems that must be addressed in regards to language testing: the training of language testing professionals and the development of standards of practice and mechanisms for implementation and enforcement. If these areas are not dealt with, language testing is not considered professionalised.

Chapter Five

Samples of Tests

5.1 English Placement Test

This placement test is designed to give English students and teachers a quick way to assess the approximate level of a student's knowledge of English grammar and usage. The test usually takes around 45 minutes to complete. At the end of the test, students view their test results and are given a percentage score. They are also able to follow a link to view an estimate of their proficiency level as compared to results from several international English examinations (PET, FCE, CAE, CPE, IELTS) and the Council of Europe Language Assessment Scale. For a more accurate assessment, listening, speaking, and writing skills must also be assessed.

1. Did you ____ anywhere interesting last weekend?
a) go
b) going
c) was
d) went

2. I work as a teacher and my wife ____ too.
a) do
b) is
c) work
d) does

3. I think ____ taxi driver
a) her job
b) she's a
c) her job is an
d) she's

4. What is your home town ____?
a) situated
b) age
c) like
d) located

5. I'm afraid I ___ here for your birthday party.
a) have not to be
b) am not being
c) will be not
d) can't be

6. How ___ are you?
a) high
b) wide
c) long
d) heavy

7. How long ___ married?
a) have you been
b) are you
c) have you
d) been

8. Would you like ___ help?
a) a
b) some
c) me
d) I

9. They ____ go to the cinema
a) tomorrow
b) much
c) rare
d) seldom

10. He hasn't played since he ____ the accident.
a) had
b) has had
c) has
d) had had

11. This is the best tea I have ____ tasted.
a) never
b) ever
c) already
d) still

12. I am looking ____ the summer holidays.
a) before
b) forward
c) for
d) forward to

13. My girlfriend ____ born on the 2nd of September, 1974.
a) is
b) was
c) had
d) has been

14. This beer tastes ____.
a) badly
b) lovely
c) well
d) normally

15. In life, ____ can make a mistake; we are all human.
a) anyone
b) some people
c) not anybody
d) someone

16. She knows that she ____ to pay now.
a) had better
b) needn't
c) should
d) ought

17. If he ____ about it, I'm sure he would help.
a) had know
b) knew
c) has known
d) knows

18. I will return the newspaper when I ____ through it.
a) will have looked
b) looked
c) have looked
d) look

19. They said they ____ come, but they didn't.
a) can
b) will
c) may
d) might

20. They were ____ hard questions that I had no chance.
a) so
b) some
c) such
d) quite

21. I don't have a cent to give you. I ____ bought a new computer.
a) just buy
b) had just bought
c) 've just
d) soon will

22. Mum gave ____ her job when I was born.
a) in
b) up
c) off
d) away

23. It's all right. We ____ hurry. We have plenty of time.
a) mustn't
b) shouldn't
c) can't
d) needn't

24. You have a terrible fever! ____ call a doctor?
a) Shall I
b) Do I
c) Must I
d) Will I

25. Joanna looks ____ in her new dress.
a) nice
b) nicely
c) like nice
d) such nice

26. Mr Haines wants ____ to his office.
a) that you come
b) you come to
c) you come
d) you to come

27. There are ____ around to start a cricket team.
a) enough young boys
b) boys enough young
c) young boys enough
d) enough youngest boys

28. These bottles ____ of plastic.
a) are making
b) are make
c) are made
d) made are

29. Do you know where ____?
a) did I put the keys
b) put I the keys
c) I put the keys
d) I the keys put

30. Magda knows a lot about badgers, but she ____ a live one.
a) doesn't ever see
b) hasn't ever seen
c) hasn't ever saw
d) didn't ever see

31. We wash the curtains ____ year.
a) three times a
b) once
c) three every
d) every couple

32. The loud speakers won't work unless you ____ those cables.
a) connected
b) connect
c) don't connect
d) can't connect

33. You should give ____.
a) to your mother this letter
b) this letter your mother
c) letter this to your mother
d) this letter to your mother

34. Marian has ____ old books.
a) very much
b) a lot of
c) lots
d) a very a lot

35. Hania has got two children, ____?
a) hasn't she
b) she has got
c) has she
d) haven't she

36. Let's think ____ something nice.
a) after
b) about
c) for
d) to

37. A jaguar is ____ than a flat.
a) more expensive
b) expensive
c) much expensive
d) expensive

38. The TV's too loud. Please ____.
a) it turns down
b) turn it up
c) turn it down
d) turn down it

39. It's a pity you ____ here last night.
a) weren't
b) aren't
c) 'll not be
d) 'd not be

40. What about ____ for a walk?
a) to go
b) I going
c) going
d) go

41. I made one or two mistakes, but ____ of my answers were correct.
a) much
b) most
c) more
d) few

42. You can't cross the road when the light ____ red.
a) 'll be
b) was
c) were
d) is

43. I have a problem. ____ help me, please?
a) Could you
b) Should you
c) Were you able to
d) Will you able

44. Our neighbour is ___ to Ireland.
a) going travel
b) going to travelling
c) go
d) going to travel

45. Do penguins fly? No, they ___.
a) aren't
b) haven't
c) don't
d) won't

46. ___ train are you taking? The express to Poznań or to Skwierzyna?
a) Which
b) How
c) Whose
d) Who

47. This is ___ story.
a) a very interesting
b) very an interesting
c) very interesting
d) very interested

48. Marta takes the dog for a walk ____ the evening.
a) in
b) at
c) on
d) to

49. We haven't got ____ Polish friends.
a) no
b) any
c) none
d) some

50. Simon can't ____ to you now. He's busy.
a) talked
b) to talk
c) talking
d) talk

51. Have they finished working yet? I don't think ____.
a) it
b) this
c) so
d) that

52. Somebody stole his wallet, so he ____ money from a friend.
a) lent
b) earned
c) borrowed
d) landed

53. We must go now. Call the waitress and ask for the ____.
a) bill
b) invoice
c) price
d) cost

54. He's a friend of ____.
a) them
b) threes
c) theirs
d) their

55. Have you had ____ to eat?
a) too many
b) some more
c) to many
d) enough

56. I ___ my boyfriend since Christmas.
a) didn't see
b) haven't seen
c) don't see
d) hasn't seen

57. Who was the woman ___?
a) spoke to
b) that you were speaking to
c) that you spoke
d) that you were speaked

58. Is ___ than his father?
a) Matt taller
b) Taller Matt
c) Matt more tall
d) Matt as tall as

59. She was twenty-nine on her birthday, ___ she?
a) didn't
b) hadn't
c) hasn't
d) wasn't

60. ____ is it from here to Berlin?
a) How long way
b) How long
c) How far
d) How many

61. Good ____! I hope you get the job.
a) chance
b) fortune
c) luck
d) wish

62. The doctor has told her that she must give ____ drinking.
a) from
b) to
c) off
d) up

63. There was a lot of noise, so I didn't understand what she was ____.
a) saying
b) telling
c) speaking
d) talking

64. I ___ drink beer than wine.
a) would like more
b) prefer
c) had better
d) would rather

65. I gave her ___ earrings for Christmas.
a) a pair of
b) a set of
c) two
d) a

66. Would like some more tea? There's still ___ left.
a) few
b) a few
c) a little
d) little

67. She didn't want the job, ___.
a) how well paid was it
b) how well paid it was
c) for how good pay might it be
d) however good pay it was.

68. He has been ____ for armed robbery.
a) blamed
b) accused
c) charged
d) arrested

69. The financial director ____ almost an hour.
a) kept us to wait
b) kept us waiting
c) made us to wait
d) made us waiting

70. I have often ____ at the Wujec Palace Hotel.
a) stayed
b) sleeped
c) remained
d) rested

71. I didn't realise that the coffee shop was ____ the other side of the road.
a) by
b) for
c) on
d) in

72. We have ____ for a receptionist but haven't appointed anyone yet.
a) advertised
b) announced
c) advised
d) noticed

73. She is very beautiful, but that kind of woman doesn't ____ to me.
a) fancy
b) appeal
c) attract
d) turn on

74. The language school that I attend is twenty kilometres ____.
a) far
b) away
c) distance
d) long

75. 'I am going to the cinema on Saturday.'
'So ___.'
a) I am
b) do I
c) I do
d) am I

76. They ___ him for scratching the car.
a) blamed
b) accused
c) punished
d) arrested

77. They had to leave the flat because they couldn't pay the ___.
a) fare
b) hire
c) rent
d) salary

78. She ___ at me and then turned away.
a) viewed
b) regarded
c) responded
d) glanced

79. The bookshop rang ____ that the dictionary you ordered has arrived.
a) to say
b) to tell
c) for saying
d) for telling

80. If he hadn't drunk so much, he ____ sick.
a) didn't feel
b) wouldn't feel
c) hadn't felt
d) hasn't felt.

81. Maria has two sisters, but she doesn't speak to ____ of them.
a) both
b) any
c) either
d) neither

82. Hubert is an uncle of ____.
a) Kim
b) Kims
c) Kim's
d) Kims'

83. We discussed the house plans ____ our way to the shops.
a) by
b) on
c) in
d) to

84. George goes to ____ by car.
a) a work
b) the work
c) an work
d) work

85. Have you found a job ____?
a) soon
b) still
c) longer
d) yet

86. My boots are dirty. I 'd better take them ____ before I come in.
a) off
b) away
c) on
d) up

87. What did the man say ____?
a) at you
b) to you
c) for you
d) you

88. 'Do you think I should move to Ireland?'
'You shouldn't do anything ____ you think it's the right thing to do.'
a) when
b) unless
c) in case
d) if

89. We can finish the rest of the eggs for ____.
a) a breakfast
b) the breakfast
c) breakfast
d) a breakfasts

90. If she doesn't ____ my sight at once, I will scream!
a) go out from
b) go off
c) get away from
d) get out of

5.2 English Proficiency Test

5.2.1 English Grammar: Part I
Select the best answer.

1. Juan ____ in the library this morning.
a) is study
b) studying
c) is studying
d) are studying

2. Alicia, ____ the windows please. It's too hot in here.
a) opens
b) open
c) opened
d) will opened

3. The movie was ____ the book.
a) as
b) as good
c) good as
d) as good as

4. Eli's hobbies include jogging, swimming, and ____.
a) to climb mountains
b) climbs mountains
c) to climb
d) climbing mountains

5. Mr Hawkins requests that someone ____ the data by fax immediately.
a) sent
b) sends
c) send
d) to send

6. Who is ____, Marina or Sachiko?
a) tallest
b) tall
c) taller
d) the tallest

7. The concert will begin ____ fifteen minutes.
a) in
b) on
c) with
d) about

8. I have only a ____ Christmas cards to write.
a) few
b) fewer
c) less
d) little

9. Each of the Olympic athletes ____ for months, even years
a) have been training
b) were training
c) has been training
d) been training

10. Maria ____ never late for work.
a) am
b) are
c) were
d) is

11. The company will upgrade ____ computer information systems next month.
a) there
b) them
c) it's
d) its

12. Chery likes apples, ____ she does not like oranges.
a) so
b) for
c) but
d) or

13. You were ____ the New York office before 2 pm.
a) suppose call
b) supposed to call
c) supposed calling
d) supposed call

14. When I graduate from college next June, I ____ a student here for five years.
a) will have been
b) have been
c) has been
d) will have

15. Ms Guth ____ rather not invest that money in the stock market.
a) has to
b) could
c) would
d) must

5.2.2 English Grammar
Select the word or phrase that is incorrect.
The majority to the news is about is about violence or scandal.
a) the
b) to
c) news
d) violence

Takeshi swimmed one hundred laps in the pool yesterday.
a) swimmed
b) hundred
c) in
d) yesterday

When our vacation, we plan to spend three days scuba diving.
a) when
b) plan
c) days
d) diving

Mr. Feinauer does not take critical of his work very well.
a) does
b) critical
c) his
d) well

Yvette and Rinaldo send e-mail messages to other often.
a) and
b) send
c) other
d) often

6. Mr Olsen is telephoning a American Red Cross for help.
a) is
b) a
c) Red
d) for

7. I had a enjoyable time at the party last night.
a) a
b) time
c) at
d) last

8. The doctor him visited the patient's parents.
a) the
b) him
c) visited
d) patient's

9. Petra intends to starting her own software business in a few years.
a) intends
b) starting
c) software business
d) few

10. Each day after school, Jerome run five miles.
a) each
b) after
c) run
d) miles

11. He goes never to the company softball games.
a) never
b) the
c) softball
d) games

12. Do you know the student who books were stolen?
a) do
b) know
c) who
d) were

13. Jean Pierre will spend his vacation either in Singapore nor the Bahamas.
a) will
b) his
c) nor
d) Bahamas

14. I told the salesman that I was not interesting in buying the latest model.
a) told
b) that
c) interesting
d) buying

15. Frederick used work for a multinational corporation when he lived in Malaysia.
a) used work
b) multinational
c) when
d) lived in

5.2.3 English Vocabulary
Select the best answer.

1. The rate of ____ has been fluctuating wildly this week.
a) money
b) bills
c) coins
d) exchange

2. The bus ____ arrives late during bad weather.
a) every week
b) later
c) yesterday
d) always

3. Do you ____ where the nearest grocery store is?
a) know
b) no
c) now
d) not

4. Jerry Seinfeld, the popular American comedian, has his audiences ____.
a) putting too many irons in the fire
b) keeping their noses out of someone's business
c) rolling in the aisles
d) going to bat for someone

5. The chairperson will ____ members to the subcommittee.
a) appoint
b) disappoint
c) disappointment
d) disappointed

6. The critics had to admit that the ballet ____ was superb.
a) procrastinate
b) performance
c) pathology
d) psychosomatic

7. Peter says he can't ____ our invitation to dinner tonight.
a) angel
b) across
c) accept
d) almost

8. We were ____ friends in that strange but magical country.
a) upon
b) among
c) toward
d) in addition to

9. The hurricane caused ____ damage to the city.
a) extend
b) extended
c) extensive
d) extension

10. Many cultures have special ceremonies to celebrate a person's ____ of passage into adulthood.
a) right
b) rite
c) writ
d) write

5.2.4 English Reading Comprehension
Select the best answer.

Directions to Erik's House:
Leave Interstate 25 at exit 7S. Follow that road (Elm Street) for two miles. After one mile, you will pass a small shopping centre on your left. At the next set of traffic lights, turn right onto Maple Drive. Erik's house is the third house. It's number 33, and it's white with green trim.

1. What is Erik's address?
a) Interstate 25
b) 2 Elm Street
c) 13 Erika Street
d) 33 Maple Drive

2. Which is closest to Erik's house?
a) The traffic lights
b) The shopping centre
c) Exit 7S
d) A greenhouse

Date: 16 May 1998
To: Megan Fallerman
From: Steven Roberts
Subject: Staff Meeting

Please be prepared to give your presentation on the monthly sales figures at our upcoming staff meeting. In addition to accurate accounting of expenditures for the monthly sales, be ready to discuss possible reasons for fluctuations as possible trends in future customer spending. Thank you.

3. The main focus of the presentation will be ___.
a) Monthly expenditures
b) Monthly salary figures
c) Monthly sales figures
d) Staff meeting presentation

4. Who will give the presentation?
a) The company president
b) Megan Fallerman
c) Stevens Roberts
d) Future customers

The B&B Tour:
Spend ten romantic days enjoying the lush countryside of Southern England. The counties of Devon, Dorset, Hampshire, and Essex invite you to enjoy their castles and coastlines, their charming bed and breakfast inns, their museums, and their cathedrals. Spend lazy days watching the clouds drift by, or spend active days hiking the glorious hills. These fields are home to Thomas Hardy and ports that have launched ships that have shaped world history. Our tour begins 15 August. Call or

fax us today for more information: 1-800-222-x. Enrolment is limited, so please contact us soon.

5. Which of the following counties is not included in the tour?
a) Devon
b) Cornwall
c) Essex
d) Hampshire

6. How many people can go on this tour?
a) 10
b) An unlimited number
c) 2-8
d) A limited number

7. What can we infer about this area of southern England?
a) The region has lots of vegetation
b) The coast often a harsh weather
c) The sun is hot and air is dry
d) The land is flat

Anna Szewcyzk, perhaps the most popular broadcaster in news media today, got her start in journalism as an editor at the *Hollsville County Times* in Missouri. Soon, a colleague persuaded her to enter the field of broadcasting. She moved to Oregon to begin a master's degree in broadcast journalism at Atlas University. Following graduation, she was able to begin her career as a local newscaster with WPSU-TV in Seattle, Washington and rapidly advanced to national television. Noted for her quick wit and trenchant commentary, her name has since become synonymous with *Good Day, America!* Accepting the award at the National Convention of Broadcast Journalism held in Chicago, Ms Szewcyzk remarked, 'I am so honoured by this award that I'm at a total loss for words.' Who would ever have believed it?

8. What is the purpose of this announcement?
a) To invite people to the National Convention Broadcast Journalism
b) To encourage students to study broadcasting
c) To recognize Ms. Szewcyzk's accomplishments
d) To advertise a job opening at *Hollsville County Times*

9. The expression 'to become synonymous with' means ____.
a) To be same as
b) To be the opposite of
c) To be in sympathy with
d) To be discharged from

10. What was Ms Szewczyk's first job in journalism?
a) She was a TV announcer Washington
b) She was a newscaster in Oregon
c) She was an editor for a newspaper in Missouri
d) She was a talk show host in Chicago

Summary and Conclusion

In the prelude, we have tried to trace the challenges encountered by learners of foreign languages, English included. Due to the current status of English as the global language of science, technology, and international relations, many countries around the world consider learning English a major educational priority.

On the other hand, many linguists argue that learning English as a second or foreign language is often concerned with social and political interests raised by non-native learners, speakers, and writers. English as a foreign language education is now offered not only at post-secondary level but also in many high schools and junior schools around the world. Interest in English learning has increased drastically in recent years.

The idea of formal tests of knowledge and ability emerged in traditional China, where they were used to select individuals who would go on to be trained to become members of the ruling elite. Tests, thus, played a crucial role in constructing the fundamental character of Chinese cultural and political life over many centuries. Today, language tests are used throughout the world to control the entry of students into university settings where the language of instruction is not a student's first language. Language tests are also used as a form of border control, featuring as part of entry procedures to other countries.

This book has discussed a handful of English proficiencies, English proficiency tests, and other variable types of tests. It has also elaborated on English testing for specific purposes, such as grammar testing, vocabulary testing, writing testing, reading comprehension testing, method testing, and oral ability testing. Test qualities—reliability, construct validity, authenticity, interactiveness, impact, and practicality—are also included in the discussion. Measurement and evaluation, testing and evaluation, assessment and evaluation, test development processes, tests classifications, test characteristics, and other tests used in language testing have been also discussed. The book ends with chapter five, which provides samples of variable tests, followed by a summary and conclusion.

References

Alderson, J.C. & North, B. (1991). *Language Testing in the 1990s: The Communicative Legacy.* MacMillan Publishers Limited.

Al-Medani, M.A. (2005). *Testing in ESP: An Analytic Study.* [Master's thesis, Sudan University of Science and Technology]. SUST Repository. http://repository.sustech.edu/handle/123456789/8193.

Al-Sabateen, I. M.A. (2008). *Effect of Lexical, Grammatical and Cultural Background on Reading Comprehension.* [Master's thesis, Sudan University of Science and Technology]. SUST Repository. http://repository.sustech.edu/handle/123456789/8172.

Bachman, L. F. (1990). *Fundamental Consideration in Language Testing.* Oxford University Press.

Bachman, L. F. & Savignon, S. J. (2011). The Evaluation of Communicative Language Proficiency: A Critique of ACTFL Oral Interview. *The Modern Language Journal, 70,*(4), 380-399. https://www.jstor.org/stable/326817?seq=1.

Davies, A. (1968). *Language Testing Symposium: A Psycholinguistic Approach.* Oxford University Press.

ElTommy, N. E. A. (2007). *An Evaluation of Grammatical Components: A Case Study of 2 Science Textbooks (English for Libya).* [Master's thesis, Sudan University of Science & Technology]. SUST Repository. http://repository.sustech.edu/bitstream/handle/123456789/8340/An%20Evaluation%20of%20Grammatical%20...pdf?sequence=1&isAllowed=y.

Garri, D. S. A (2004). *EFL Vocabulary Learning Investigating Third Year Students Vocabulary Learning Strategies at some Sudanese Universities in the Capital Khartoum.* [Master's theses, College of Languages.] SUST Repository. http://repository.sustech.edu/handle/123456789/7986.

Harris, D. P. (1969). *Testing English as a Second Language.* TATA McGraw-Hill Publishing Company Limited.

Hamayel, M. & Atallah, M. (2008). *Investigating Strategies for Improving University Student Reading Efficiency in English.* [Master's thesis, Sudan University of Science & Technology]. SUST Repository. http://repository.sustech.edu/handle/123456789/8177.

Hughes, A. (1989). *Testing for Language Teachers.* Press Syndicate of the University of Cambridge.

Hughes, A. & Porter, A. (1983). *Current Developments in Language Testing.* Academic Press Inc.

Jin, Y. (2010). The Place of Language Testing and Assessment in the Professional Preparation of Foreign Language Teachers in China. *Language Testing, 27*(4), 555-584. https://journals.sagepub.com/doi/10.1177/0265532209351431#articleCitationDownloadContainer.

Lado, R. (1965). *Language Testing the Construction and Use of Foreign Language Tests.* Longmans, Green and Company Limited.

Omran, S. A. R. (2005). *English Language Examination System, Secondary School Certificate in Qatar.* [Master's, Sudan University of Science and Technology]. SUST Repository. http://repository.sustech.edu/handle/123456789/8092?show=full.

Richards, J., Platt, J., & Webber, H. (1985). *Longman Dictionary of Applied Linguistics.* Longman Group UK Limited.

Sawaki, Y., Lawerence, Stricker, L. J., & Oranje, A. H. (2009). Factor Structure of the TOEFL Internet-Based Test. *Language Testing,* 26(1), 5-30. https://journals.sagepub.com/doi/10.1177/0265532208097335.

Appendices

Appendix A: Types of English Proficiencies Used in This Book
    i) Language Proficiency
    ii) English Language Proficiency
    iii) English Language Proficiency and Academic Language Proficiency
    iv) English Proficiency and its Relation to Academic English
    v) Foreign Language Proficiency
    vi) Foreign Proficiency Guidelines
    vii) Communicative Language Proficiency

Appendix B: English Language Proficiency Tests
    i) English Language Proficiency Tests
    ii) IDEA Proficiency Tests
    iii) Maculattis Test of Proficiency
    iv) Stanford English Proficiency Test

Appendix C: Types of Placement Tests
    i) Placement Testing
    ii) Global Placement Test
    iii) Placement Tests as Adaptive Tests

    iv) Placement Testing as an Essential Ingredient
    v) Placement Testing: Who Should Be Tested?
    vi) Placement Test Selection

Appendix D: Tests and Testing
    i) Tests
    ii) Tests and Examinations
    iii) Direct and Indirect Tests
    iv) Subjective and Objective Tests
    v) Tests and Quizzes
    vi) Oral and Written Tests

Appendix E: Objective Tests
    i) True and False Tests
    ii) Multiple-Choice Tests
    iii) Matching Tests

Appendix F: Norm-Referenced Tests versus Criterion-Referenced Tests
    i) Norm-Referenced Tests
    ii) Criterion-Referenced Tests

Appendix G: Testing
   i) Testing English for Specific Purposes
   ii) Testing Method
   iii) Testing Grammar
   iv) Testing Vocabulary
   v) Testing Reading Comprehension
   vi) Testing Oral Ability
   vii) Testing Writing

Appendix H: Test Qualities
   i) Reliability
   ii) Construct Validity
   iii) Authenticity
   iv) Interactiveness
   v) Impact
   vi) Practicality

Appendix I: Measurement and Evaluation
   a) i) Measurement
      ii) Evaluation
   b) i) Assessment
      ii) Evaluation

Appendix J: The Test Development Process
    i) Design
    ii) Operationalisation
    iii) Administration

Appendix K: Classification of Tests
Venkates Waran (1950) classifies tests into the following categories:

    i) Knowledge Tests as Contrasted with Performance or Skill Tests
    ii) Subjective and Objective Tests
    iii) Productive and Receptive Tests
    iv) Language Skill Tests and Communicative Skill Tests
    v) Proficiency Tests and Achievement Tests

Appendix L: Characteristics of a Good Test
    i) Content validity
    ii) Predictive validity
    iii) Concurrent validity
    iv) Reliability
    v) Discrimination
    vi) Backwash
    vii) Objectivity
    viii) Scorability
    ix) Practicability

Appendix M: Early Work on Language Tests, Language Testing, and Language Proficiency

i) Morante (1986) worked on language testing and defined placement testing as a term used in higher education to describe a process of student assessment, the results of which are used to place college students in appropriate beginning courses.

ii) McNamara (1991) elucidates that language testing has undergone a rapid evolution in past 50 years, mirroring the development of applied linguistics broadly.

iii) Fairbank and Goldman (1998) argue that language tests have played a crucial role in constructing the fundamental character of Chinese cultural and political life, starting many centuries ago.

iv) Dutton (1998), Jones (1998), and McNamara (2001) explain the use of language tests in border control, reflecting on histories of arriving immigrants who were deemed undesirable on racial grounds and were subjected to tests of 100 words in a language they didn't know, ultimately failing.

v) Bachman (2000) illustrates that language testing emerged as a discipline and established its status as a branch of applied linguistics in the 1990s.

vi) Jin (2010) designed a questionnaire to investigate the provision and instruction of language testing and assessment courses at tertiary level and to identify areas for improvement.

vii) Hughes and Porter (1983) discuss three important developments in language testing: research directed at investigating the structure of foreign language ability, approaches to devising reliable and valid measures of communicative competence, and growth in the number of tests designed to test language for specific purposes.

viii) Cummins (1980) argues that English language proficiency is not a dichotomous process, instead developing along a continuum. Social English proficiency takes approximately two to three years to develop, whereas academic English proficiency takes approximately five to seven years to develop.

ix) Word-Class Instructional Design and Assessment (WIDA) (2004) demonstrates that proficiency is an advance towards completeness for perfection—improvement in skills or knowledge.

x) Freed (1987) describes foreign language proficiency as an ability to perform all the language modalities (listening, writing, and speaking), and an understanding of the cultural framework of the language being studied.

xi) Green and Weir (2004) elaborate, stating that placement testing is an area that has received little attention in language testing research.

xii) According to Morante (1987), nine factors should be considered in any decision about a particular placement test. These include in-house testing, test content, referencing, discrimination, speediness, reliability, validity, and cost.

xiii) Morante (1986) states that a placement test, or a battery of tests, is essential in determining which courses or levels of courses are appropriate for individual students.

xiv) Morante (1986) also says that colleges must place as much emphasis on the careful selection of a placement test as they do on curriculum development and student recruitment.

xv) Pilliner (1968) argues that a test is a measuring device used to compare an individual to other individuals belonging to the same group.

www.ingramcontent.com/pod-product-compliance
Lightning Source LLC
Chambersburg PA
CBHW030259010526
44107CB00053B/1758